My Body

My Stomach

by Rena Korb

illustrated by Rémy Simard

Content Consultant:
Anthony J. Weinhaus, PhD
Assistant Professor of Integrative Biology and Physiology
University of Minnesota

magic
wagon

visit us at www.abdopublishing.com

Published by Magic Wagon, a division of the ABDO Group, 8000 West 78th Street, Edina, Minnesota, 55439. Copyright © 2011 by Abdo Consulting Group, Inc. International copyrights reserved in all countries. All rights reserved. No part of this book may be reproduced in any form without written permission from the publisher.

Looking Glass Library™ is a trademark and logo of Magic Wagon.

Printed in the United States of America, North Mankato, Minnesota.
022010
092010

 THIS BOOK CONTAINS AT LEAST 10% RECYCLED MATERIALS.

Text by Rena Korb
Illustrations by Rémy Simard
Edited by Holly Saari
Interior layout and design by Emily Love
Cover design by Emily Love

Library of Congress Cataloging-in-Publication Data
Korb, Rena B.
  My stomach / by Rena Korb ; illustrated by Remy Simard ; content consultant, Anthony J. Weinhaus.
     p. cm. — (My body)
  Includes index.
  ISBN 978-1-60270-810-5
  1. Stomach—Juvenile literature. 2. Digestion—Juvenile literature. I. Simard, Rémy, ill. II. Weinhaus, Anthony J. III. Title.
  QP151.K67 2011
  612.3'2—dc22
                        2009048330

Table of Contents

My Stomach

Hi! I'm Jonas. I ate a turkey sandwich for lunch. Now I'm full. Let's find out what our stomachs do after we fill them up!

How did the sandwich get to my stomach in the first place? After I swallowed it, it went down a long tube called the esophagus. This tube connects my mouth to my stomach.

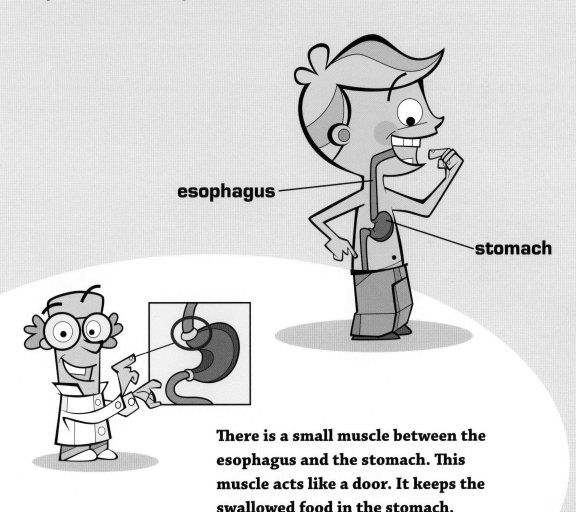

esophagus

stomach

There is a small muscle between the esophagus and the stomach. This muscle acts like a door. It keeps the swallowed food in the stomach.

My stomach is just below my ribs. It becomes busy when I eat. My stomach helps digest food. It breaks swallowed food into smaller bits.

You might rub your belly when you have a stomachache. But that is not where the stomach is located. The stomach is much higher.

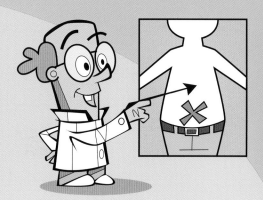

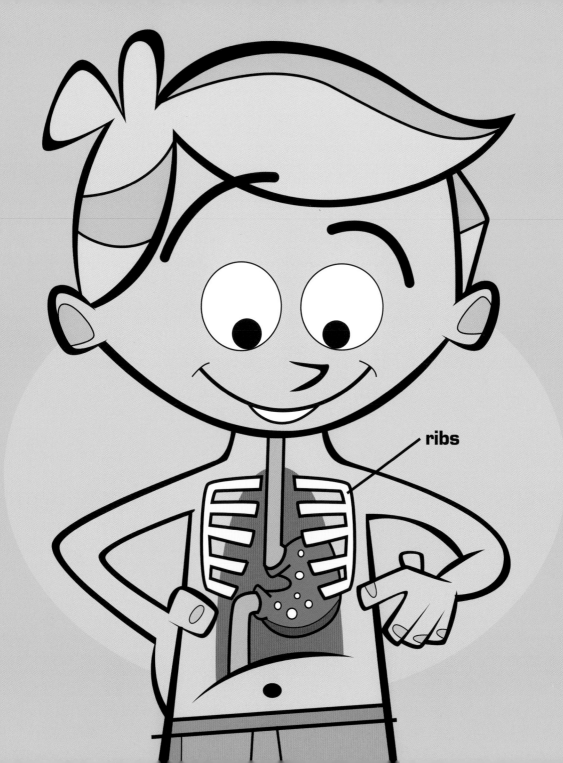

ribs

My stomach digests food so my body can use it. Food gives my body energy. This energy helps me run, jump, and think.

Food also gives the body nutrients. They help your bones grow and your body stay healthy.

My stomach is like a balloon. It is smaller than a fist when it's empty. It stretches when I fill it with food.

You stomach grows as you do! A newborn's stomach is about the size of a marble. But the average adult stomach is about the size of one quart (.95 L) of milk.

empty

full

Let's look inside my stomach. Check out my sandwich. It's so mushy! That's because I already chewed it. But it's still not mushy enough for my body to use. My stomach must get to work!

People can get stomachaches from:
• eating too much food,
• eating food too quickly,
• eating food that has bad germs.

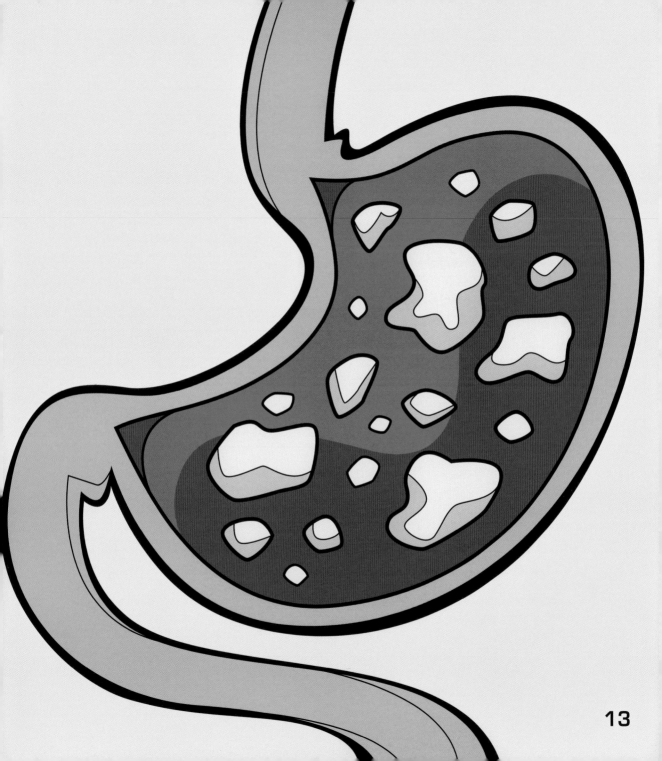

13

My stomach has strong muscles. Squeeze! They move the food around and mash it up.

Your stomach's muscles can squeeze when it's empty. You hear your stomach growl!

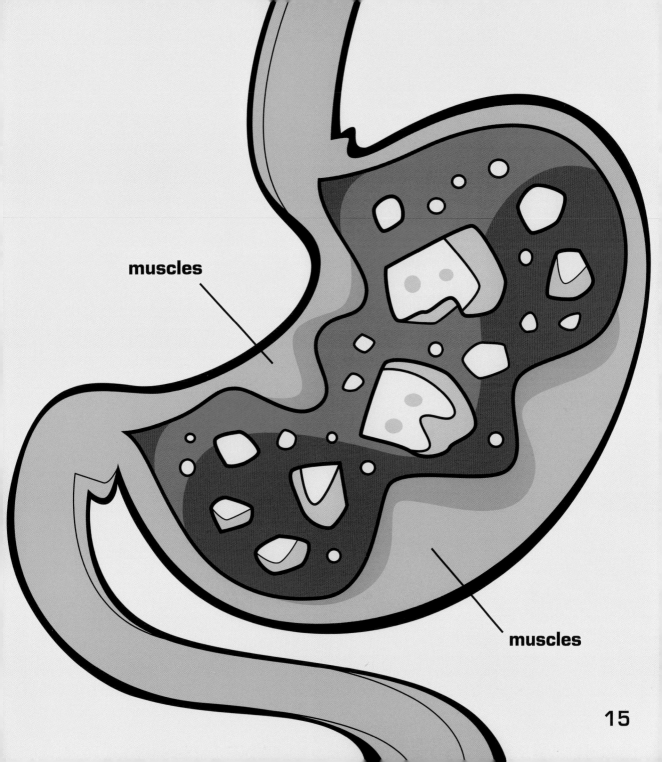

muscles

muscles

My stomach makes special juices. They break the food into even smaller pieces.

Your stomach makes juices even when it's empty. It makes juices when you see, smell, or think about food.

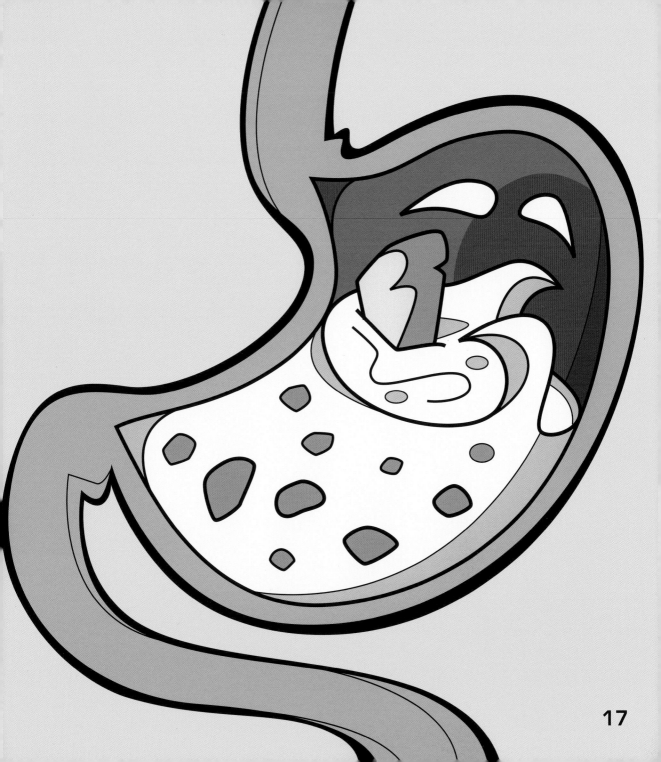

My stomach keeps working. It makes my sandwich soupy. My turkey sandwich stays in my stomach for as long as five hours.

Drink lots of water. That helps the body digest food.

The stomach breaks down some foods faster than others. The bread in my sandwich gets broken down faster than the turkey.

Besides bread and turkey, the stomach breaks down other foods at different speeds. Fruits are broken down faster than fried foods.

My stomach has a muscle at its bottom end that acts like a door. When my sandwich is broken down enough, my stomach pushes it out this door. Off the food goes to my small intestine!

Humans usually eat three meals a day. Some animals do not eat that much. Many snakes eat one meal every few months!

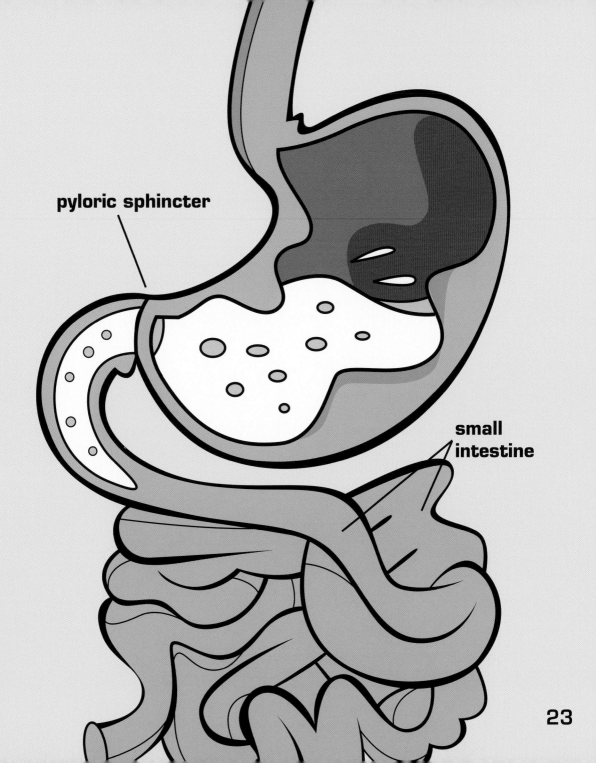

pyloric sphincter

small intestine

23

The small intestine keeps digesting my sandwich. The nutrients in the food go into my blood. My blood carries the nutrients to every part of my body.

The small intestine is not small at all. An adult's is about 20 feet (6 m) long. It is one and a half inches (4 cm) wide.

My body cannot use some parts of my sandwich. This solid waste moves into my large intestine. The waste leaves my body when I poop.

Your body makes liquid waste, too. It's called urine, or pee.

It takes my body a whole day to digest my turkey sandwich. By then, I have already eaten more meals. My stomach is hard at work with each one!

The body makes gas when it digests food. It gets rid of this gas with burps or farts.

A Look Inside

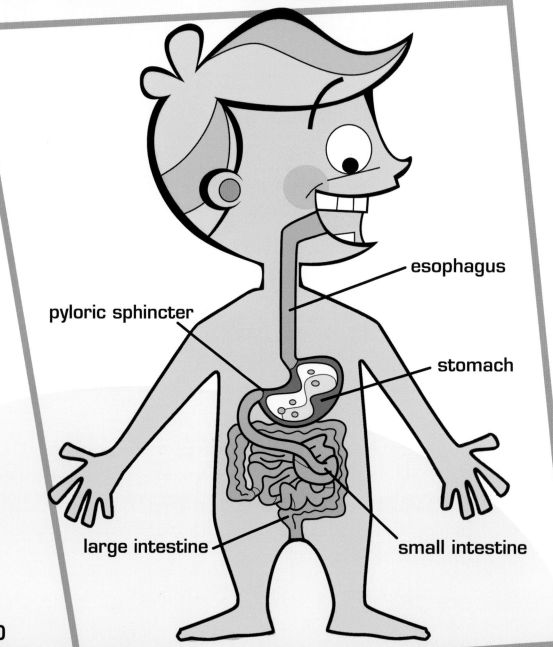

esophagus

pyloric sphincter

stomach

large intestine

small intestine

Fun Facts

- The walls of the stomach can fold up like an accordion. This happens when the stomach is empty.

- Digestive juices in the stomach do more than help digest food. They kill the germs in food that could make you sick.

- All animals have stomachs. But some animals have very different stomachs from humans. Cow and sheep stomachs have four different sections!

Glossary

digest – to break food down so that it can be used by the body.

energy – the strength needed to do activities.

esophagus (ih-SAH-fuh-gus) – the tube that takes food from the mouth to the stomach.

large intestine – the part of the body where waste waits to be removed from the body.

muscles – body parts that help the body move.

nutrients – things in food that help keep the body healthy and growing.

small intestine – the part of the body where food's nutrients are sent into the blood.

On the Web

To learn more about the stomach, visit ABDO Group online at www.abdopublishing.com. Web sites about the stomach are featured on our Book Links page. These links are routinely monitored and updated to provide the most current information available.

Index